Creative VEGETARIA Cooking

Creative vegetarian cooking means producing meals that are tasty, nutritious and so beautifully presented that even committed carnivores find them hard to resist.

Becoming a vegetarian has never been simpler. In recognition of the growing numbers, even the smaller supermarkets are starting to stock appropriate products, and the range of specialist foods is increasing steadily. Products like Worcestershire sauce, which used to be taboo because of the anchovies it contained, are now on sale in vegetarian versions, and alternatives for gelatine, an animal product, include agar-agar in powdered and flaked forms and a new carageenan derivative, which, like conventional gelatine, is available in handy sachets. The number of vegetarian cheeses (produced without the use of rennet) is also increasing.

As with any sensible eating regime, it is variety that is the key to a healthy vegetarian diet. However, if you are concerned about which foods to eat and which to avoid, seek advice from one of the specialist organisations or a dietitian. Vegans should plan with particular care.

Whether you are a staunch vegetarian, a cook who regularly caters for vegetarian friends or family, or simply someone who enjoys the occasional meat-free meal, Creative Vegetarian Cooking *provides the very best in green cuisine.*

CONTENTS

SIMPLY DELICIOUS SOUPS

Vegetarians have the pick of the crop when it comes to soups.
Take fresh country vegetables, a few carefully chosen herbs and
spices, and what have you got? Quite simply – pots of flavour!

Iced Tomato Soup

1kg (2lb) tomatoes, peeled, seeded and quartered

300ml (10fl oz) vegetable stock

1 tblspn tomato purée

dash Tabasco sauce

salt and pepper

1 tblspn finely chopped fresh basil

1 tblspn finely chopped fresh parsley

1 Place tomatoes in a saucepan with vegetable stock. Bring to the boil over moderate heat.

2 Stir in tomato purée and Tabasco, with salt and pepper to taste. Lower heat and simmer for 20 minutes.

3 Cool, then blend in a food processor or blender. Pour into a bowl, cover and refrigerate for at least 4 hours.

4 Serve soup in chilled dishes, garnishing each portion with a sprinkling of mixed basil and parsley.
Serves 4

Garlic Soup

3 tblspn olive oil

2-3 cloves garlic, crushed

4 slices bread, crusts removed, crumbled

1/2 tspn cayenne pepper

1 1/2 litres (2pt) vegetable stock

2 sticks celery, cut into matchsticks

1 parsnip, cut into matchsticks

2 eggs, beaten

3 tblspn chopped fresh parsley

salt

freshly ground black pepper

1 Heat oil in a saucepan over moderate heat. Add garlic, lower heat and cook for 2 minutes. Add bread and fry until golden. Stir in cayenne.

2 Add stock and bring to boil. Lower heat and simmer for 20 minutes. Add vegetable matchsticks. Cook for 2 minutes.

3 Add eggs and parsley to the simmering soup. Stir over heat until eggs form threads. Season to taste and serve at once.
Serves 4

Spicy Pumpkin Soup

30g (1oz) butter

1 large onion, chopped

1kg (2lb) pumpkin, cubed

900ml (1 1/2pt) vegetable stock

1/2 tspn grated nutmeg

125ml (4fl oz) evaporated milk

salt

freshly ground black pepper

1 Melt butter in a large saucepan. Add onion and cook for 3-4 minutes, until golden. Add pumpkin cubes and cook for 2 minutes more, stirring constantly.

2 Add stock and nutmeg. Bring to boil, then simmer until pumpkin is tender.

3 Purée soup in batches. Return to clean pan and stir in the evaporated milk. Season with salt and pepper and more nutmeg if desired. Reheat without boiling.
Serves 4-6

Spicy Pumpkin Soup

Hearty Vegetable Soup

220g (7oz) dried lima beans or butter beans, soaked overnight in water to cover

2 tblspn sunflower oil

1 leek, sliced

1 large Spanish onion, sliced

2 large cloves garlic, finely chopped

1 large carrot, sliced

6 fresh button mushrooms, finely chopped

4 tomatoes, peeled, seeded and chopped

1 turnip, cut into 1cm (1/2in) cubes

1 parsnip, cut into 1cm (1/2in) cubes

1 large potato, cut into 1cm (1/2in) cubes

350g (11oz) cabbage, shredded

5 sticks celery, sliced

2 tblspn chopped fresh parsley

2 tblspn chopped fresh basil or marjoram

2 litres (3 1/2pt) vegetable stock

salt

freshly ground black pepper

1 Drain beans, rinse them under cold water and drain again. Place in a large saucepan with enough water to cover, bring to boil and boil for 10 minutes. Lower heat, cover and cook for 1-1 1/4 hours or until beans are tender. Drain.

2 Heat oil in a very large saucepan. Add leek, onion and garlic. Sauté for 5 minutes. Add carrot, mushrooms, tomatoes, turnip, parsnip, potato, cabbage, celery and herbs. Sauté for 5 minutes, stirring constantly. If mixture is too dry, add a little of stock.

3 Add remaining stock. Bring to boil, simmer for 30 minutes or until vegetables are tender.

4 Stir in cooked beans and cook for 10 minutes or until heated through. Season to taste.
Serves 12

Green Minestrone

60g (2oz) butter

250g (8oz) fresh asparagus

500g (1lb) broccoli

4 spring onions, chopped

155g (5oz) thawed frozen or fresh broad beans

220g (7oz) thawed frozen or fresh peas

2 vegetable stock cubes

155g (5oz) green beans, topped and tailed

1 Melt butter in a large saucepan over moderate heat. Set aside the asparagus tips; chop the stalks and add them to the pan.

2 Set aside the broccoli florets for use in another recipe; chop the stems and add them to the pan with the spring onions, broad beans and 155g (5oz) of the peas.

Toss lightly to mix; cook until just softened.

3 Crumble in the stock cubes. Add enough water to cover the vegetables by 2.5cm (1in). Bring to the boil, lower the heat and simmer until all the vegetables are tender.

4 Purée the soup in several batches in a blender or food processor. Return the purée to the clean pan, add the reserved asparagus tips, remaining peas and green beans and cook for 5 minutes more. Serve in heated bowls with fresh bread rolls.
Serves 4

Kitchen Tip
Sprue – green asparagus spears which are too thin for canning and therefore available at a very reasonable price from farm shops and markets – are ideal for this soup.

Green Minestrone

Leek Soup with Thyme

30g (1oz) butter

350g (11oz) leeks, white part only, chopped

2 potatoes, chopped

2 tspn chopped fresh thyme, plus extra for garnish

1 litre (1³/4pt) vegetable stock

4 tblspn single cream

1 Melt butter in a large saucepan over moderate heat. Add leeks and cook for 2 minutes. Add potatoes and thyme; toss to coat in butter.

2 Add stock. Bring to boil, then simmer until potatoes are tender. Purée mixture, return to clean pan and heat through.

3 Serve soup in heated bowls. Spoon one tablespoon of cream onto centre of each portion, swirling it with a skewer. Garnish with fresh thyme.
Serves 4

Red Lentil Soup

2 tblspn olive oil

2 onions, finely chopped

2 carrots, finely chopped

1 tspn curry powder

1 tspn ground cumin

1/4 tspn chilli powder

2cm (³/4in) piece fresh root ginger, grated

220g (7oz) red lentils, rinsed and drained

1 litre (1³/4pt) vegetable stock

1 Heat oil in a large saucepan. Add the onions and carrots and cook for 5 minutes over moderate heat, stirring occasionally. Stir in dry spices and ginger; cook for 1 minute.

2 Add lentils and stock. Bring to boil, lower heat and simmer, covered, for 30 minutes or until lentils are very soft.

3 Purée mixture, return to clean pan, heat through without boiling.
Serves 4

Leek Soup with Thyme

Courgette and Coriander Soup

15g (¹/2oz) butter

1 large onion, chopped

6 large lettuce leaves stripped from the outside of an Iceberg lettuce, shredded

185g (6oz) courgettes, roughly chopped

90g (3oz) fresh coriander, leaves stripped from stems

750ml (1¹/4pt) vegetable stock

salt

freshly ground black pepper

185ml (6fl oz) cream or fromage frais

2 tblspn chopped fresh coriander

1 Melt butter in a large saucepan, add onion and sauté until golden. Add lettuce leaves, courgettes and coriander leaves; sauté for 3 minutes.

2 Add stock. Bring to boil, lower heat and simmer until vegetables are tender. Purée mixture and transfer to a large bowl. If mixture is too thick, stir in extra stock or water. Season to taste. Chill.

3 Stir in cream or fromage frais. Serve in chilled bowls, topped with chopped coriander.
Serves 6

Fennel Soup

2 tblspn olive oil

1 onion, sliced

1 clove garlic, crushed

4 fennel bulbs, trimmed

1 x 397g (13oz) can chopped tomatoes

2 tblspn tomato purée

1 litre (1³/₄pt) vegetable stock

salt

freshly ground black pepper

1 long loaf crusty Italian bread to serve

1 Heat oil in a large saucepan. Add onion and garlic and cook over gentle heat for 5 minutes, stirring occasionally.

2 Halve fennel bulbs. Set aside feathery tops for garnish; slice fennel thinly. Add to pan with tomatoes. Stir in tomato purée; cook for 5 minutes over moderate heat.

3 Add stock. Bring to boil, lower heat and simmer, covered, for 30 minutes. Add salt and pepper to taste.

4 Meanwhile preheat oven to 180°C (350°F/Gas 4). Cut bread into 2cm (³/₄in) slices. Arrange on a baking sheet; bake for 20 minutes, turning halfway through, until golden.

5 Ladle soup into heated bowls, garnish with fennel tops and serve with toasted Italian bread.

Serves 4

Minestrone

2 tblspn olive oil

1 onion, chopped

1 clove garlic, crushed

1 carrot, chopped

2 courgettes, chopped

1 stick celery, sliced

2 potatoes, chopped

185g (6oz) drained canned cannellini beans or red kidney beans, rinsed

1 x 400g (14oz) can chopped tomatoes with basil

1 tspn dried oregano

4 tblspn tomato purée

1 litre (1¾pt) vegetable stock

125g (4oz) cabbage, shredded

125g (4oz) small pasta shapes

2 tblspn chopped fresh parsley

grated Parmesan cheese to serve

1 Heat oil in a large saucepan. Add onion and garlic and cook over gentle heat for 5 minutes, stirring occasionally.

2 Add carrot, courgettes, celery and potatoes, tossing vegetables in oil. Cook for 5 minutes, stirring occasionally.

3 Add beans, tomatoes and oregano. Mix well. Stir tomato purée into vegetable stock, then stir mixture into pan. Bring to boil, lower heat and simmer, covered, for 30 minutes.

4 Add cabbage and pasta to soup; cook for about 7 minutes, or until pasta is tender. Stir in parsley.

5 Serve in heated bowls, with plenty of Parmesan.
Serves 4

Kitchen Tip
Buy fresh Parmesan in the piece if possible and grate it on the fine side of a grater. A small amount goes a long way, and the flavour is much better than the prepackaged product.

Carrot Soup with Ginger

1 tblspn sunflower oil

1 small onion, finely chopped

1 clove garlic, crushed

2 tspn finely grated fresh root ginger

250g (8oz) carrots, sliced

600ml (1pt) vegetable stock

juice of 2 limes

1 Heat oil in a saucepan. Add onion, garlic and ginger and cook over moderate heat for 3-4 minutes, until golden.

2 Add carrots and stock. Bring to boil, then simmer until carrots are tender.

3 Purée mixture with lime juice in a blender or food processor. Either return soup to clean pan and reheat gently or scrape purée into a bowl and chill until required.
Serves 4

Chestnut Soup

125g (4oz) butter

1 onion, roughly chopped

2 carrots, roughly chopped

30g (1oz) plain flour

2 litres (3½pt) vegetable stock

500g (1lb) canned chestnuts, drained

salt

freshly ground black pepper

250ml (8fl oz) single cream (optional)

1 Melt butter in a saucepan. Add onion and carrots and cook over gentle heat for 5 minutes.

2 Stir in flour and cook for 1 minute. Raise heat and gradually add stock, stirring until mixture thickens slightly. Add chestnuts, with salt and pepper to taste. Simmer, uncovered, for 30 minutes.

3 Purée soup. Return to clean pan, add cream if using, and reheat gently. Serve in heated bowls.
Serves 8

Fennel Soup

Carrot and Dill Soup

Miso Soup

Miso is available from health food shops.

2 tblspn olive oil

1 onion, chopped

1 clove garlic, crushed

1 stick celery, sliced

1 carrot, chopped

1 parsnip, chopped

1 orange-fleshed sweet potato, chopped

90g (3oz) piece pumpkin, chopped

90g (3oz) drained canned or thawed frozen sweetcorn

500ml (16fl oz) vegetable stock

8 tspn miso

1 Heat oil in a large saucepan. Add onion and garlic and cook over gentle heat for 5 minutes, stirring occasionally.

2 Add celery, carrot, parsnip, sweet potato, pumpkin and corn. Cook for 5 minutes more, stirring occasionally.

3 Add stock. Bring to boil, lower heat and simmer, covered, for 30 minutes.

4 Place 2 teaspoons miso in each of four heated soup bowls. Ladle in hot soup and serve.
Serves 4

Pear and Celery Soup

90g (3oz) butter

1 large onion, roughly chopped

6 sticks celery, sliced

1.5 litres (2¹/₂pt) vegetable stock

2 tblspn white wine

750g (1¹/₂lb) pears, peeled, cored and chopped

125ml (4fl oz) single cream

salt

freshly ground black pepper

1 Melt butter in a saucepan. Add onion and cook over gentle heat until pale gold in colour. Add celery, cover pan and cook until celery is tender.

2 Add stock and bring to boil. Lower heat, add wine and simmer, covered, for 30 minutes.

3 Add pears. Simmer for 20 minutes, or until pears are tender. Remove pan from the heat. Cool slightly and purée until smooth.

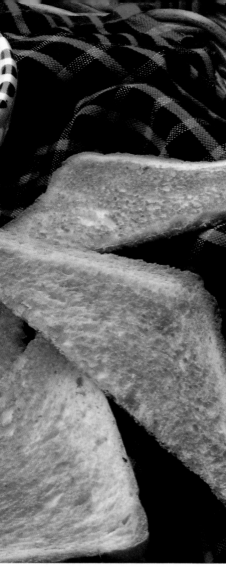

Creamy Mushroom Soup

4 Strain through a sieve into clean pan. Stir in cream and season to taste. Reheat gently without boiling. Serve in heated bowls, garnished with a chopped celery leaf if liked.

Serves 6

Carrot and Dill Soup

30g (1oz) butter

1 large onion, chopped

1 large orange-fleshed sweet potato, chopped

3 large carrots, sliced

1 litre (1³/₄pt) vegetable stock

185ml (6fl oz) soured cream

2 tblspn chopped fresh dill

1 Melt butter in a saucepan. Add onion, sweet potato and carrots; sauté for 5 minutes.

2 Stir in vegetable stock. Bring to boil, lower heat and simmer for 30 minutes or until vegetables are tender.

3 Purée mixture with soured cream. Return to clean pan and reheat gently without boiling. Stir in dill and serve at once, in heated bowls.

Serves 4

Creamy Mushroom Soup

60g (2oz) butter

1 large onion, sliced

375g (12oz) button mushrooms, sliced

1 tblspn chopped fresh chervil

500ml (16fl oz) vegetable stock

2 tblspn cornflour

250ml (8fl oz) milk

125ml (4fl oz) double cream

1 Melt butter in a large saucepan. Add onion and mushrooms; sauté for 5 minutes.

2 Add chervil and stock. Simmer for 20 minutes. Purée in a blender or food processor. Return mixture to clean pan.

3 In a cup, mix cornflour to a paste with a little of milk. Add to mushroom purée with the remaining milk. Stir over moderate heat until soup boils and thickens. Off heat, stir in cream. Serve at once, garnished as desired.

Serves 4

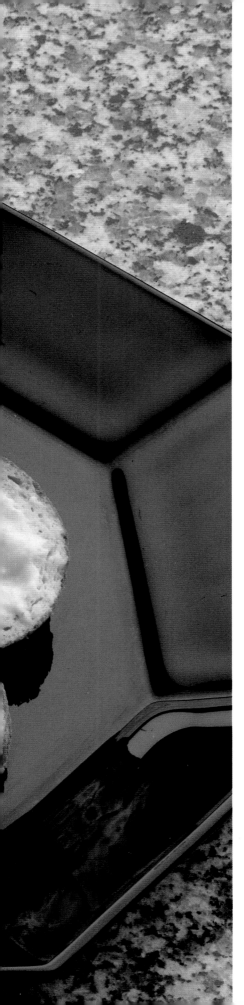

Take a fresh look at the first course with this mouthwatering selection. Mangetout Mousse, Harlequin Tomatoes, Courgette Roulade — vegetarians starved of variety need look no further.

Courgette Roulade

125g (4oz) courgettes, grated

2 tblspn water

4 eggs, separated

2 tblspn grated Gruyére cheese

3 tblspn grated Parmesan cheese

1/2 tspn grated nutmeg

Filling

30g (1oz) butter

30g (1oz) plain flour

300ml (10fl oz) milk

185g (6oz) ricotta cheese

1 Make filling. Melt butter in a medium saucepan over moderate heat. Add flour and cook for 1 minute. Gradually add milk, stirring until sauce boils and thickens. Set aside 3 tablespoons of the sauce in a large bowl for roulade. Stir the ricotta into remaining sauce. Cover surface of sauce with dampened greaseproof paper and set aside until required.

2 Preheat oven to 190°C (375°F/ Gas 5). Line and grease a 30 x 25cm (12 x 10in) Swiss Roll tin. Combine grated courgettes and measured water in a small saucepan. Cook over moderate heat until soft; drain thoroughly and pat dry between two sheets of paper towel. Stir cooked courgette into sauce in large bowl. Add the egg yolks, grated cheeses and nutmeg and mix well. Beat egg whites in a grease-free bowl until stiff; fold into courgette mixture.

3 Pour mixture into tin and smooth the surface. Bake for 12-15 minutes or until the surface springs back when pressed lightly.

4 Turn roulade out onto a wire rack covered with a clean tea-towel.

5 Roll up roulade with tea-towel; hold for 30 seconds, then unroll. Carefully peel off lining paper and remove tea-towel. Cool for 10-15 minutes, spread evenly with cheese filling and roll up again. Serve sliced, at room temperature.
Serves 6

Celeriac Crudité

4 tblspn mayonnaise

2 tspn Dijon mustard

2 tspn white wine vinegar

1/4 tspn salt

1 celeriac, cut into thin matchsticks

4 slices wholegrain bread, toasted

chopped fresh parsley for garnish

1 Combine the mayonnaise, mustard, vinegar and salt in a bowl. Mix to a smooth paste.

2 Stir in the celeriac. Spread thickly on the hot toast, cut into quarters or fingers and arrange on individual plates. Sprinkle with parsley and serve at once.
Serves 4

Courgette Roulade

Cheddar Soufflé

Mangetout Mousse

250g (8oz) mangetout, trimmed
155ml (5fl oz) water
2 tspn finely chopped onion
2 tspn agar-agar
2 tblspn chopped fresh parsley
1 tblspn snipped chives
salt
freshly ground black pepper
½ tspn lemon juice
155ml (5fl oz) natural low fat yogurt
1 egg white, stiffly beaten
Melba toast to serve

1 Set aside 8 mangetout for garnish. Heat 125ml (4fl oz) of water in a small saucepan, add the remaining mangetout and onion and cook over moderate heat until tender. Meanwhile mix agar-agar to a smooth cream with remaining water.

2 Transfer mangetout mixture to a blender or food processor; add parsley, chives and agar-agar and process until smooth. Stir in salt and pepper to taste; add lemon juice. Cover and refrigerate.

3 When purée is on point of setting, fold in yogurt. Beat egg white in a grease-free bowl until stiff; fold into purée.

4 Rinse four ramekins with cold water; shake dry. Divide mangetout mixture evenly between ramekins. Refrigerate for at least 4 hours or until set.

5 Lightly cook the reserved mangetout. Serve moulds on individual plates, with mangetout garnish. Offer Melba Toast separately.
Serves 4

Kitchen Tip
To make Melba toast, toast thinly sliced bread. Cut off crusts. Carefully cut each slice of toast in half to make two very thin slices from each; place under a hot grill, untoasted sides uppermost, until golden brown and curling at the edges.

Cheddar Soufflé

60g (2oz) butter
60g (2oz) plain flour
300ml (10fl oz) hot milk
125g (4oz) mature Cheddar cheese, grated
1 tspn grated nutmeg
3 eggs, separated
2 tblspn snipped chives, plus whole chives for garnish
1 red pepper, cut into strips
2 carrots, cut into strips
2 courgettes, cut into strips
125g (4oz) broccoli florets

1 Preheat oven to 180°C (350°F/ Gas 4). Melt butter in a saucepan over moderately low heat.

2 Stir in flour and cook for 1 minute. Gradually add hot milk, stirring constantly until mixture boils and thickens. Remove from heat, stir in cheese and transfer to a large bowl. Cool for 10 minutes.

3 Stir in nutmeg, egg yolks and chives. Mix well. Beat egg whites in a grease-free bowl until soft peaks form. Fold into cheese mixture, adding about 4 tablespoons at a time.

4 Divide mixture between six greased and collared individual soufflé dishes or ramekins. Bake for 15-20 minutes.

5 Meanwhile, cook vegetables in a large saucepan of boiling water until crisp-tender. Drain and serve with soufflés. Garnish with whole chives.
Serves 6

Warm Broccoli Mousse

45g (1¹/₂oz) butter, softened

2 medium heads broccoli, florets and stems separated

2 eggs

125ml (4fl oz) single cream

salt

freshly ground black pepper

Lemon Butter Sauce

2 tblspn lemon juice

4 tblspn single cream

250g (8oz) butter, cut into 2cm (³/₄in) cubes

1 Preheat oven to 190°C (375°F/ Gas 5). Grease six individual soufflé dishes or ramekins with softened butter.

2 Bring a saucepan of water to boil, add broccoli and cook for 10 minutes or until tender. Drain, refresh under cold water and drain again.

3 Purée broccoli. Add eggs and cream and process to combine. Season to taste.

4 Spoon mixture into prepared dishes. Place in a roasting tin and pour in enough hot water to come halfway up the sides of the dishes. Bake for 1 hour.

5 Make sauce: reduce lemon juice by half in a small saucepan over moderately low heat. Add cream and bring to boil. Whisk in butter, one cube at a time. Do not let pan get too hot; lift it from time to time and keep whisking away from heat. When all butter has been added, season to taste.

6 Invert mousses onto individual plates. Spoon sauce over and around mousses and serve at once.
Serves 6

Fresh Asparagus Polonaise

16 green asparagus spears, trimmed

60g (2oz) butter, melted

2 hard-boiled eggs, chopped

60ml (2fl oz) double cream

¹/₄ tspn grated nutmeg

fine pepper strips for garnish

1 Bring a tall, deep saucepan of water to boil. Stand asparagus spears upright in water so that stems are submerged but tips cook in steam. Cook until stems are tender.

2 Make sauce: blend or process melted butter with chopped eggs, cream and nutmeg until smooth. Transfer mixture to a small saucepan and heat through.

3 Drain asparagus thoroughly and arrange on individual plates. Spoon sauce over top and garnish with red pepper strips. Serve at once.
Serves 4

Kitchen Tip

Asparagus can also be steamed in a wok. Lay the spears on a rack over simmering water, arranging them so that the tips point away from the centre. Cover the wok and steam until tender.

Fresh Asparagus Polonaise

Summer Vegetable Pâté

30g (1oz) butter

2 tblspn olive oil

1 onion, finely chopped

1 head celery, leaves only, finely chopped

3 spring onions, finely chopped

500g (1lb) spinach, leaves stripped from stems, roughly chopped and washed

4 tblspn chopped fresh parsley

2 tblspn chopped fresh oregano or basil

1/4 tspn sugar

2 tblspn lemon juice

salt

freshly ground black pepper

8 slices white bread, crusts removed

250ml (8fl oz) milk

1kg (2lb) courgettes, cut into 2.5cm (1in) slices

2 eggs plus 2 yolks

30g (1oz) fresh white breadcrumbs

tomato slices for garnish

1 Preheat oven to 180°C (350°F/ Gas 4). Melt butter in olive oil in a saucepan. Add onion, celery leaves and spring onions. Cook for 5 minutes or until soft.

2 Place spinach in a separate saucepan, cover and cook until spinach is tender. Shake pan frequently. Drain spinach, refresh under cold water and drain again. Squeeze to remove excess moisture. Add to the saucepan containing onion.

3 Stir in herbs and sugar. Cook over very low heat for 15 minutes, stirring occasionally, add lemon juice. Season to taste. Transfer mixture to a blender or food processor; process briefly to a coarse purée. Spoon into a large bowl.

4 Soak bread slices in milk in a shallow bowl for 5 minutes. Squeeze out excess moisture and crumble bread into spinach purée.

5 Cook courgettes, drain and purée. Tip purée into a sieve

lined with a clean tea-towel and press out as much moisture as possible. Add to spinach mixture.

6 Whisk eggs and yolks together in a bowl; stir into spinach mixture.

7 Lightly butter a loaf pan; sprinkle with three quarters of the breadcrumbs. Pour spinach mixture into pan. Butter a piece of foil, sprinkle with remaining breadcrumbs and invert it on top of pan to cover pâté.

8 Bake for 1¹/4 hours, then remove foil and bake for 15 minutes more until golden on top. Turn off heat and leave pâté to cool in oven for 1 hour.

9 Turn pâté onto a platter and cool completely. Wrap in foil and refrigerate for at least 4 hours, preferably overnight. Garnish with tomato slices.

Serves 8

Harlequin Tomatoes

2 tblspn mayonnaise

4 large tomatoes, each cut into three 1cm (¹/2in) slices

12 slices mozzarella cheese, cut into rounds

6 slices peeled cucumber, halved

6 pitted black olives, halved

flat-leaf parsley for garnish

Pesto

30g (1oz) fresh basil leaves

1 clove garlic, roughly chopped

30g (1oz) pinenuts

2 tblspn olive oil

2 tblspn grated Parmesan cheese

1 Make pesto: place all ingredients in a blender or food processor and blend until smooth. Stir in mayonnaise.

2 Arrange tomato slices on a platter. Top with pesto mayonnaise. Add a mozzarella slice and half cucumber slice to each, and garnish with the olives and parsley.

Serves 4-6

Harlequin Tomatoes

SNACKS AND SUPPERS

The old adage about a little of what you fancy doing you good really does apply when it comes to vegetarian snacks and suppers. Dishes like Stuffed Red Peppers, Bulgur Pilaf or Crustless Broccoli and Leek Quiche are both nutritious and tasty.

Baked Macaroni with Tomatoes

3 large ripe tomatoes
salt
500g (1lb) macaroni
30g (1oz) butter
250g (8oz) mozzarella, thinly sliced
60g (2oz) grated Parmesan cheese
freshly ground black pepper

1 Preheat oven to 190°C (375°F/ Gas 5). Cut tomatoes into 5mm (¼in) slices. Place in a colander and sprinkle with salt. Stand in sink for 30 minutes to drain.

2 Cook macaroni in a large saucepan of lightly salted water until just tender, see Kitchen Tip. Drain, transfer to a bowl and toss with half the butter.

3 Layer half the tomatoes in a buttered ovenproof serving dish. Add a layer of half the mozzarella slices, cover with half the macaroni and sprinkle half the Parmesan on top. Repeat the layers, ending with Parmesan.

4 Season with plenty of black pepper, dot with the remaining butter and bake for 30 minutes or until the topping is golden brown. Serve hot.

Serves 6

Kitchen Tip
The macaroni should retain quite a bit of 'bite' after boiling as it will continue to cook in the oven.

Aubergines Stuffed with Black-eyed Beans

3 medium aubergines
90ml (3fl oz) oil
1 onion, chopped
125g (4oz) cooked black-eyed beans or red kidney beans
125g (4oz) cooked long-grain brown or white rice
3 tomatoes, chopped
2 tblspn chopped fresh parsley
2 tblspn chopped fresh dill
salt
freshly ground black pepper
300ml (10fl oz) ragu (thick tomato sauce)
60g (2oz) grated Parmesan cheese

1 Preheat oven to 190°C (375°F/ Gas 5). Cut aubergines in half lengthwise. Scoop out flesh, taking care not to damage shells. Cube the flesh.

2 Heat oil in a large saucepan. Add onion and aubergine cubes; stir fry for 5 minutes. Add beans, rice, tomatoes and herbs, season to taste. Mix well. Fill aubergine shells with mixture.

3 Arrange the filled aubergine shells side by side in two shallow ovenproof dishes. Pour in boiling water to come halfway up the sides of the aubergines. Bake for 1 hour.

4 Drain off water from dishes. Top each aubergine with ragu and sprinkle with Parmesan. Return to oven for 20 minutes or until cheese has melted.

Serves 6

Stuffed Red Peppers

Stuffed Red Peppers

3 red peppers

90g (3oz) wholemeal breadcrumbs

4 spring onions, chopped

1 large carrot, grated

2 courgettes, grated

2 sticks celery, finely chopped

2 cloves garlic, crushed

60g (2oz) hazelnuts, chopped

125ml (4fl oz) natural low fat yogurt

2 tblspn wheatgerm

30g (1oz) matured Cheddar cheese, grated

1 Preheat oven to 180°C (350°F/ Gas 4). Cut peppers in half lengthwise, remove seeds and pith.

2 Combine breadcrumbs, spring onions, carrot, courgettes, celery, garlic, nuts and yogurt in a bowl. Spoon into pepper shells. Place on a baking sheet and bake for 30 minutes or until peppers are tender.

3 Sprinkle with wheatgerm and cheese; bake for 10 minutes more or until cheese has melted. Serve at once.

Serves 6

Celery Flan

Gnocchi alla Romana

250ml (8fl oz) vegetable stock

750ml (1¼pt) milk

90g (3oz) butter

155g (5oz) cornmeal

250ml (8fl oz) water

155g (5oz) grated Parmesan cheese

¼ tspn grated nutmeg

1 Bring stock and milk to boil in a large saucepan over moderate heat. Add 30g (1oz) of butter and stir until melted.

2 Mix cornmeal and measured water to a smooth paste in a bowl. Slowly pour mixture into the milk, stirring until mixture is smooth and very thick.

3 Line a large shallow pan with greaseproof paper. Pour in cornmeal mixture. Smooth surface and cool completely.

4 Preheat oven to 180°C (350°F/ Gas 4.) Grease baking tin with 15g (1½oz) of remaining butter. Cut out 4cm (1½in) rounds of cornmeal mixture with a biscuit cutter; fold each round in half.

5 Arrange gnocchi in tin. Melt remaining butter and pour over gnocchi. Sprinkle with Parmesan and nutmeg. Bake for 20-25 minutes until golden.

Serves 6

Bulgur Pilaf with Spring Onions

6 spring onions, white and green parts separated

2 tblspn oil

1 tspn ground cumin

155g (5oz) bulgur wheat

375ml (12fl oz) water

1 tspn salt

1 Slice white part of spring onions thinly. Slice sufficient of green stems to measure 4 tablespoons. Keep separate.

Celery Flan

250g (8oz) shortcrust pastry, thawed if frozen

30g (1oz) butter

1 onion, finely chopped

5 stalks celery, finely chopped

1 green pepper, finely chopped

2 tblspn finely chopped spring onion

2 tblspn plain flour

375ml (12fl oz) milk

60ml (2fl oz) single cream

2 eggs

½ tspn crushed black peppercorns

1 Preheat oven to 190°C (375°F/ Gas 5). On a floured surface, roll out pastry to fit a 20cm (8in) flan dish. Ease pastry into dish, prick base and bake for 10 minutes. Set aside.

2 Melt butter in a saucepan. Add onion, celery, green pepper and spring onion and cook over moderate heat for 10 minutes.

3 Stir in flour and cook for 1 minute. Gradually add milk, stirring until mixture boils and thickens slightly. Remove from heat.

4 Cover top of sauced vegetables with dampened greaseproof paper to prevent formation of a skin. Cool sauce to room temperature.

5 Reheat oven to 180°C (350°F/ Gas 4). Beat cream, eggs and black pepper into the sauced vegetables. Pour mixture into the pastry case. Bake for 35 minutes.

Serves 6

2 Heat oil in a small heavy-based saucepan. Add cumin and white part of spring onions and cook over low heat until soft, stirring constantly. Stir in bulgur and cook for 1 minute.

3 Add measured water and salt. Bring to boil, cover pan and lower heat to a bare simmer. Cook for 10-15 minutes or until all liquid has been absorbed.

4 Remove pan from heat and stir in green part of spring onions. Replace lid and allow to stand for 5 minutes more. Fluff up the grain with a fork and serve.

Serves 4

Trasimeno Tagliatelle

125g (4oz) broccoli florets
60g (2oz) cauliflower florets
1 courgette, thinly sliced
1 small carrot, sliced diagonally in thin slices
salt
500g (1lb) tagliatelle
1 tblspn olive oil
2 spring onions, thinly sliced
1 small tomato, chopped
1/2 red pepper, chopped
1 quantity Pesto, see Harlequin Tomatoes, page 14
60g (2oz) sun-dried tomatoes in oil, drained, thinly sliced
grated Parmesan cheese to serve

1 Boil broccoli, cauliflower, courgette and carrot into a medium pan of salted boiling water. When water returns to boil, cook vegetables for 2 minutes; drain and set aside. Add tagliatelle to a larger pan of boiling water and cook until just tender.

2 Meanwhile heat oil in a frying pan over moderate heat. Add drained vegetables with spring onions, fresh tomato and pepper. Stir fry for 4 minutes or until the vegetables are crisp-tender.

3 Drain pasta and place it in a large heated bowl. Add the vegetables, pesto and sliced sun-dried tomatoes. Toss well to mix. Serve immediately. Offer the Parmesan cheese separately.

Serves 4

Tofu with Curry Sauce

3 tblspn peanut oil
2 cloves garlic, chopped
1 tblspn medium curry paste
1 tblspn soft light brown sugar
2 tblspn soy sauce
60ml (2fl oz) vegetable stock
125ml (4fl oz) creamed coconut
500g (1lb) firm tofu, cut into 2cm (3/4in) cubes
fine red pepper strips for garnish

1 Heat oil in a medium frying pan over moderate heat. Add garlic and cook for 1 minute. Stir in curry paste, sugar, soy sauce, stock and creamed coconut. Simmer for 6 minutes or until sauce starts to thicken.

2 Arrange tofu cubes on a serving plate, pour sauce over top and garnish with red pepper strips.

Serves 4

Tofu with Curry Sauce

Deep-fried Cheese Balls

1 x 200g (6½oz) tub full fat soft cheese

125g (4oz) grated Parmesan cheese

¼ tspn grated nutmeg

3 tblspn chopped fresh parsley

125g (4oz) dried breadcrumbs

1 egg, lightly beaten

oil for deep frying

parsley sprig for garnish

1 Cream soft cheese in a bowl. Add Parmesan, nutmeg, parsley and half the breadcrumbs. Stir in egg. Form mixture into small balls; roll in remaining breadcrumbs until coated on all sides.

2 Deep fry cheese balls in hot oil, turning frequently, for about 3 minutes or until evenly browned all over. Using a slotted spoon, transfer them to paper towels to drain.

3 Serve cheese balls hot or cold, garnished with parsley.

Serves 4

Buckwheat Noodles with Olive and Tomato Sauce

2 tblspn olive oil

1 large onion, finely chopped

2 cloves garlic, crushed

2 x 397g (13oz) cans chopped tomatoes with herbs

2 tblspn tomato purée

½ tspn sugar

60g (2oz) green stuffed olives, sliced

3 tblspn drained capers

280g (9oz) dry buckwheat noodles

salt

fresh basil sprigs for garnish

1 Heat oil in a saucepan. Add onion and garlic and fry over gentle heat for 5 minutes.

2 Stir in tomatoes, tomato purée, sugar, olives and capers. Bring mixture to boil over moderate heat, then simmer for 30 minutes.

3 Cook noodles in a large saucepan of boiling salted water until just tender. Drain thoroughly. Divide between six plates. Top with sauce. Serve at once, with fresh basil garnish.

Serves 6

Crustless Broccoli and Leek Quiche

2 leeks, sliced

315g (10oz) broccoli, divided into small florets

250g (8oz) Gruyére cheese, grated

2 slices day-old bread, crusts removed, diced

6 eggs, lightly beaten

¼ small onion, finely chopped

¼ tspn grated nutmeg

salt

freshly ground black pepper

100ml (3½fl oz) soured cream

1 Preheat oven to 180°C (350°F/ Gas 4). Steam leeks over boiling water for 6 minutes. Add broccoli and steam for 1 minute more. Refresh under cold water, drain and set aside.

2 Mix cheese, bread, eggs, onion and nutmeg in a bowl. Stir in salt and pepper to taste. Add the soured cream. Add leeks and broccoli and mix lightly.

3 Spoon mixture into a buttered quiche dish. Bake in centre of oven for about 30 minutes or until a knife inserted in quiche comes out clean. Serve at once.

Serves 6

Buckwheat Noodles with Olive and Tomato Sauce, Deep-fried Cheese Balls

Aubergine Soufflé

75g (2¹/₂oz) butter

2 cloves garlic, crushed

1 onion, finely chopped

1 large aubergine, peeled and finely chopped

75ml (2¹/₂fl oz) water

500ml (16fl oz) milk

7 eggs

2 tblspn plain flour

125g (4oz) mature Cheddar cheese, grated

1 Preheat oven to 160°C (325°F/ Gas 3). Melt 45g (1¹/₂oz) of butter in a large frying pan. Add garlic and onion and cook for 2 minutes. Stir in chopped aubergine and cook for 5 minutes more.

2 Add water to pan, cover and simmer over very low heat for 1 hour, stirring frequently and adding more water if necessary.

3 Meanwhile bring 375ml (12fl oz) of milk to boil with remaining butter. Separate 5 of the eggs; set whites aside in a grease-free bowl. Put yolks and whole eggs in a separate bowl with remaining milk. Add flour and mix well.

4 Slowly pour egg and milk mixture into boiling milk, whisking constantly. Lower heat and continue whisking until mixture thickens. Remove from heat and stir in cheese and aubergine mixture.

5 Beat egg whites until stiff; fold into aubergine mixture. Pour into a large greased soufflé dish. Bake for 35 minutes or until well risen and cooked through; serve at once.
Serves 4-6

Kitchen Tip

Before baking the soufflé, run a spoon around the surface, just inside the rim, to create a gutter. This will help to ensure that the soufflé rises evenly.

Aubergine Soufflé

Italian Gratin of Potatoes, Mushrooms and Tomatoes

375ml (12fl oz) hot water

22g (³/₄oz) dried mushrooms

3 tblspn olive oil

250g (8oz) button mushrooms, thinly sliced

salt

375g (12oz) potatoes, very thinly sliced

freshly ground black pepper

375g (12oz) tomatoes, very thinly sliced

30g (1oz) Parmesan cheese, grated

155g (5oz) mozzarella, grated or thinly sliced

1 Pour hot water over dried mushrooms in a small bowl. Allow to stand for 30 minutes. Strain through a sieve lined with a dampened clean tea-towel into a measuring jug. Reserve 155ml (5fl oz) of liquid. Rinse mushrooms, pat dry and chop finely.

2 Preheat oven to 200°C (400°F/ Gas 6). Heat 2 tablespoons of olive oil in a large frying pan. Add button mushrooms. Sprinkle with a little salt. Sauté over high heat for about 4 minutes, until mushrooms are soft. Set aside.

3 Arrange potatoes in a greased gratin dish. Spoon reserved liquid from dried mushrooms over top and sprinkle with salt and pepper to taste. Add a layer of mixed fresh and dried mushrooms; top with tomatoes. Season with more salt and pepper and drizzle remaining oil over the top.

4 Bake for about 30 minutes, or until the potatoes are just cooked.

5 Combine cheeses in a bowl. Sprinkle mixture over tomatoes. Return gratin to oven for a further 10-15 minutes, until topping is golden. Allow to stand at room temperature for 15 minutes before serving.
Serves 6

Spinach Frittata

Spinach Frittata

2 tblspn olive oil

2 cloves garlic, crushed

12 large spinach leaves, chopped

6 eggs

60ml (2fl oz) single cream

1/4 tspn grated nutmeg

freshly ground black pepper

90g (3oz) Emmental cheese, grated

1 Preheat oven to 180°C (350°F/ Gas 4). Heat oil in a frying pan. Add garlic and spinach and stir over moderate heat. The mixture will become moist as spinach releases water, but will then dry as spinach evaporates. Set aside to cool.

2 Lightly beat eggs. Add cream, nutmeg, pepper and cheese. Mix well; stir in spinach and garlic mixture. Pour into a greased 23cm (9in) flan dish. Bake for 20 minutes or until set.
Serves 4

Ricotta Roulade

250g (8oz) frozen chopped spinach, thawed

2 tspn Dijon mustard

6 eggs, separated

salt

freshly ground black pepper

410g (13oz) ricotta cheese

1 bunch chives, finely snipped

1 lemon, cut into 8 wedges, for garnish

1 Preheat oven to 190°C (375°F/ Gas 5). Line and grease a 30 x 25cm (12 x 10in) Swiss Roll tin. Cook spinach, following package directions. Drain thoroughly, tip into a bowl and cool slightly.

2 Add mustard and egg yolks to spinach and mix well. Season.

3 Beat egg whites until stiff; fold into spinach mixture. Pour mixture into tin and smooth the surface. Bake for 12-15 minutes or until surface springs back when pressed lightly.

4 Turn roulade out onto a fresh sheet of greaseproof paper; remove lining paper. Cover with ricotta and chives. Roll up gently. Serve sliced, garnished with the lemon wedges.
Serves 6-8

Green Beans with Almonds

500g (1lb) French beans, topped and tailed

60g (2oz) butter

½ onion, finely chopped

1 clove garlic, crushed

60g (2oz) flaked almonds

salt

freshly ground black pepper

1 Bring a saucepan of salted water to boil, add beans and cook until crisp-tender. Drain, refresh under cold running water and drain again.

2 Melt butter in a frying pan. Add onion and sauté until golden. Stir in garlic and almonds and cook over moderately low heat until almonds are golden. Stir in beans and heat through, stirring gently to coat beans with the mixture. Add salt and pepper to taste and serve at once.
Serves 4

French Peas

125g (4oz) butter

125ml (4fl oz) water

500g (1lb) fresh or thawed frozen peas

1 small onion, finely chopped

½ Iceberg lettuce, shredded

1 tspn sugar

salt

freshly ground black pepper

1 Melt butter in water in a large saucepan. Bring to boil. Add peas, onion, lettuce and sugar, with a pinch of salt. Cover and cook over gentle heat for 10 minutes or until peas are tender.

2 Remove lid and cook until all liquid has evaporated. Add plenty of black pepper. Serve hot.
Serves 4

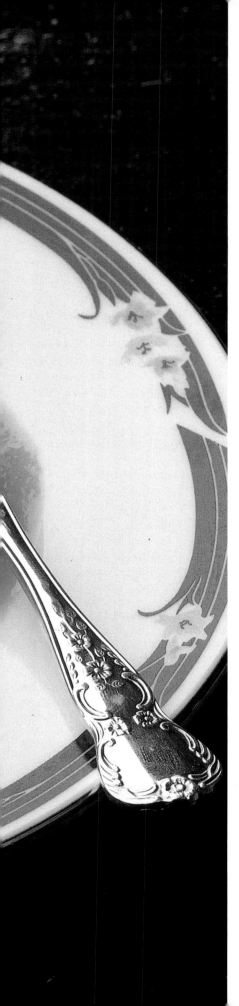

SWEET SUCCESS

There's unashamed indulgence in this collection of dessert recipes – and why not? After enjoying a ragout of vegetables, a ratatouille kebab or a celery gratin you can afford to spoil yourself with a sumptuous sweet.

Mixed Berry Meringues with Apricot Coulis

3 egg whites, at room temperature

75g (2¹/₂oz) caster sugar

1 tspn vanilla essence

90g (3oz) raspberries

90g (3oz) blueberries or pitted black cherries

3 tblspn Grand Marnier

1 x 235g (7¹/₂oz) can apricot halves, drained

60ml (2fl oz) apricot and orange nectar

6 fresh mint sprigs to decorate

1 Preheat oven to 150°C (300°F/ Gas 2). Using an electric mixer, beat egg whites in a grease-free bowl until light and fluffy. Gradually add sugar, beating all the time.

2 Add vanilla; beat for 10 minutes more until the mixture is thick and glossy.

3 Place mixture in a piping bag. Pipe six nests, about 6cm (2¹/₂in) in diameter, on a baking sheet lined with nonstick parchment.

4 Bake for 20 minutes, then lower oven temperature to 120°C (250°F/Gas 1/2); bake for 25 minutes more. Cool on baking sheet.

5 In a small bowl, combine raspberries, blueberries or cherries and Grand Marnier. Purée apricot halves with apricot and orange nectar in a blender or food processor.

Mixed Berry Meringues with Apricot Coulis

6 To assemble the dessert, spoon 2 tablespoons of apricot coulis onto each serving plate. Fill each meringue nest with berry mixture, place one nest on each plate and decorate with fresh mint. Serve at once.
Serves 6

Poached Greengages with Pear Purée

12 firm greengages

125g (4oz) caster sugar

1 tspn ground cinnamon

1 tspn grated nutmeg

¹/₂ tspn ground cloves

1 x 455g (14¹/₂oz) can pear halves, drained and chopped

2 tblspn lemon juice

2 tblspn freshly squeezed orange juice

1 tblspn finely chopped fresh mint

cinnamon sticks, to decorate

1 Place greengages in a saucepan with enough water to cover. Stir in sugar, cinnamon, nutmeg and cloves. Simmer fruit until tender but still whole. Cool in syrup.

2 Blend pears with citrus juices in a blender or food processor until smooth; stir in mint.

3 Spoon a quarter of the pear purée into each serving plate. Arrange drained greengages on top and decorate with cinnamon sticks.
Serves 4

Fluffy Chocolate Mousse

60g (2oz) butter

100g (3¹/₂oz) dark chocolate

1 tspn grated orange rind

1 tblspn Tia Maria

3 eggs, separated

60ml (2fl oz) warm water

whipped cream to decorate

1 Melt butter with chocolate in top of a double boiler over simmering water, stirring constantly.

2 Allow chocolate mixture to cool slightly; stir in orange rind and liqueur. Combine egg yolks and measured water in a bowl. Beat with a hand-held electric mixer until pale and fluffy. Fold into the chocolate mixture until well combined.

3 Beat egg whites in a grease-free bowl until stiff. Fold into the chocolate mixture. Pour into four serving glasses and refrigerate for 2 hours. Top each dessert with a swirl of cream just before serving.
Serves 4

Tart Lime Creams with Fresh Mango Sauce

oil for greasing

2 juicy limes

100ml (3¹/₂fl oz) double cream

2 large eggs

1 tblspn caster sugar

1 large ripe mango

1 Preheat oven to 180°C (350°F/ Gas 4). Lightly oil four ramekins. Pare the zest from 1 lime. Bring a small saucepan of water to boil, add lime zest and boil for 2 minutes. Drain, shred finely and set aside for garnish.

2 Combine cream and eggs in a bowl. Beat until well combined. Squeeze the limes and add the juice to egg mixture. Stir in sugar and stir well to combine.

3 Pour lime mixture into prepared moulds. Place the moulds in a roasting tin and pour in enough hot water to come halfway up sides. Bake for 25 minutes or until a skewer inserted in moulds comes out clean. Cool, then refrigerate moulds until well chilled.

4 Meanwhile, peel and stone mango. Purée flesh in a blender or food processor. Spoon mango sauce onto four dessert plates; turn out one mould on the centre of each. Garnish with reserved lime zest and serve.
Serves 4

Fluffy Chocolate Mousse

42

Layered Strawberry Burnt Cream

300ml (10fl oz) extra-thick double cream or clotted cream

250g (8oz) strawberries, hulled and halved

600ml (1pt) whipping cream

1/2 tspn vanilla essence

6 egg yolks

75g (2¹/₂oz) caster sugar

1 Spread double cream in a 25 x 20cm (10 x 8in) baking dish which can be used under grill. Place halved strawberries, cut-side down, on paper towels to blot excess juice, then arrange on top of cream.

2 Combine whipping cream and vanilla in a heavy-based saucepan. Bring to just below boiling point. Meanwhile put egg yolks in a large heatproof bowl, add 2 tablespoons of sugar and beat with an electric hand-held mixer until pale and frothy.

3 Pour scalded cream onto egg yolks, whisking constantly until combined. Place bowl over a saucepan of simmering water and stir until cream thickens. Do not allow mixture to boil. Cool custard in bowl, then carefully strain over the strawberries. Place the dish in the refrigerator for at least 8 hours, preferably overnight.

4 Dust surface of dessert with the remaining sugar, wipe sides of dish clean, and place under a pre-heated grill. The dish should be at least 10cm (4in) away from heat. Allow sugar to caramelise, see Kitchen Tip. Carefully remove from grill and allow to cool to room temperature. Do not refrigerate dessert. Serve cool.
Serves 6-8

Kitchen Tip
Do not leave the strawberry cream unattended at any time when it is under the grill. Remove it as soon as the sugar caramelises, and remember to use an oven glove as the dish will be very hot.

Dried Fruit and Nut Compote

Dried Fruit and Nut Compote

125g (4oz) caster sugar

125ml (4fl oz) water

500g (1lb) dried apricots

280g (9oz) prunes, pitted

185g (6oz) seedless raisins

125g (4oz) blanched almonds

60g (2oz) shelled pistachio nuts

2 tblspn rosewater

1 Combine sugar and water in a saucepan. Heat gently, stirring, until sugar dissolves, then add apricots, prunes and raisins. Bring liquid to boil, remove pan from heat and pour mixture into a bowl. Set aside to cool.

2 When fruit mixture is quite cold, add the blanched almonds and pistachios. Stir in rosewater. Cover bowl and refrigerate overnight. Serve plain, or with Greek yogurt, crème fraîche or double cream.
Serves 4-6

At a time when the tradition of the printed word is being constantly probed and challenged by the technology of the chip, let us marvel that the art of written expression is alive and being nurtured still, in our schools.

Six years of teaching experience with primary school children, two of which were spent as a Creative Writing Advisor for the Geraldton ~ Midlands region in Western Australia, has afforded me many opportunities to work with hundreds of teachers and thousands of children.

This book is a collection of imaginative and workable ideas, presented as a series of photocopiable sheets, all of which I have either put to use myself or have seen the practical results of, during my teaching career.

It is a smorgasbord of Creative Writing ideas.

Go ahead, sample them. They work!

Christine Syme.

Creative Writing

The pattern of creative writing falls roughly into these parts:

1. Stimulus or motivation to write.
2. Pre-writing stage ; including choice of form(s).
3. First draft.
4. Re reading - revising - editing.
5. Final copy and publication.
6. Readers' response.

Stimulus :

Providing opportunities so that children want to write — about meaningful things, things that matter!
A direct, sensory experience — tasting, doing, feeling , a film , an excursion, a competition , writing letters, making menus, sharing jokes , giving advice, reviewing books...

Well Hi-i-i-i Kiddies — ...did you hear the one about.....

Pre-Writing Stage:

An exchange period between children. Teacher,t is free to contribute own thoughts and ideas. It's a time for brainstorming all avenues of expression about a topic or idea.

　　Decide on the type of form the writing will
be — letter, poem, narrative prose, invitation,
fairytale, fantasy, diary, brochure, interview,
ballad, song,　　　　　　advertisement,
play, fable　　　　　　　horoscope, grocery list,
cartoons,
captions. etc

Gasp
NOT EXACTLY
WHAT I HAD
ENVISAGED!

The First draft:

Eliminate fear of the blank page, the fear of first
putting pen to paper, by providing a direction
or formula, a framework to work within.
The rough draft stage is a sharing time. Ideas
can be hurriedly jotted down and jumbled
around.　Perhaps compose a poem as a class,
write it on the blackboard, using contributions
from everyone.

Re reading - Revising - Editing :

Encourage children to become their own critics.
Change a sentence here, alter words and phrases there.
Teacher and child can discuss work constructively,
offering substitute words for stronger effect. Editing
means the process of altering words or reshuffling
sentences. Revising is looking back over the work
to improve grammar, spelling or punctuation.

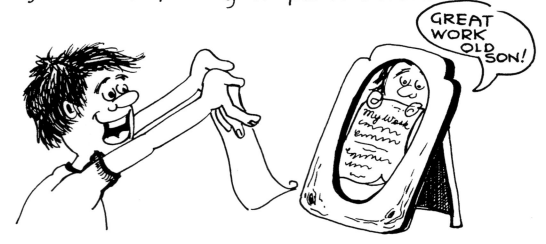

Do the sentences make sense? Does the opening
sentence grab attention? Does the title relate?
Watch for chances to re inforce the skills from
formal English lessons, into the creative writing ones.

Final Copy & Publication :

Finished work can be compiled into class books.
Every child's work may be included in the book. In
this way the child finds he is writing for a
wider audience, rather than just for the teacher,
or himself.

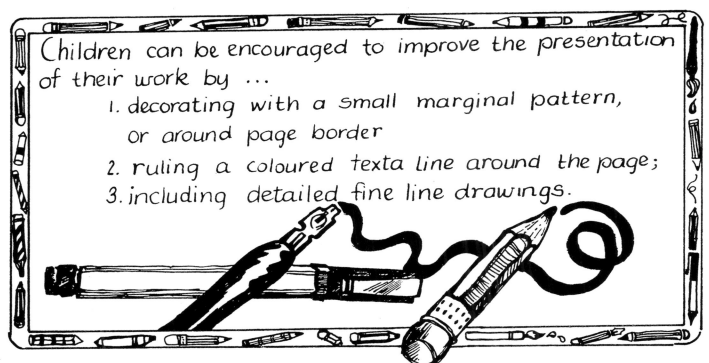

Children can be encouraged to improve the presentation of their work by ...
1. decorating with a small marginal pattern, or around page border
2. ruling a coloured texta line around the page;
3. including detailed fine line drawings.

A library of class books is soon built up and becomes the basis of a reading corner. This collection of books is an asset to the teacher who needs to assess progress individually and collectively, and to the children, it is an indication that their written works are taken notice of and enjoyed by others.

Readers' Response.

By publishing their writing in varied forms, children can enjoy the opportunity of having their work read and discussed by their peers. This in turn helps to boost their confidence and leads to a keener awareness of the importance of their own beliefs, thoughts, feelings and efforts.

By encouraging your students to share their work with others, you will be helping them to develop a positive attitude to the written word.

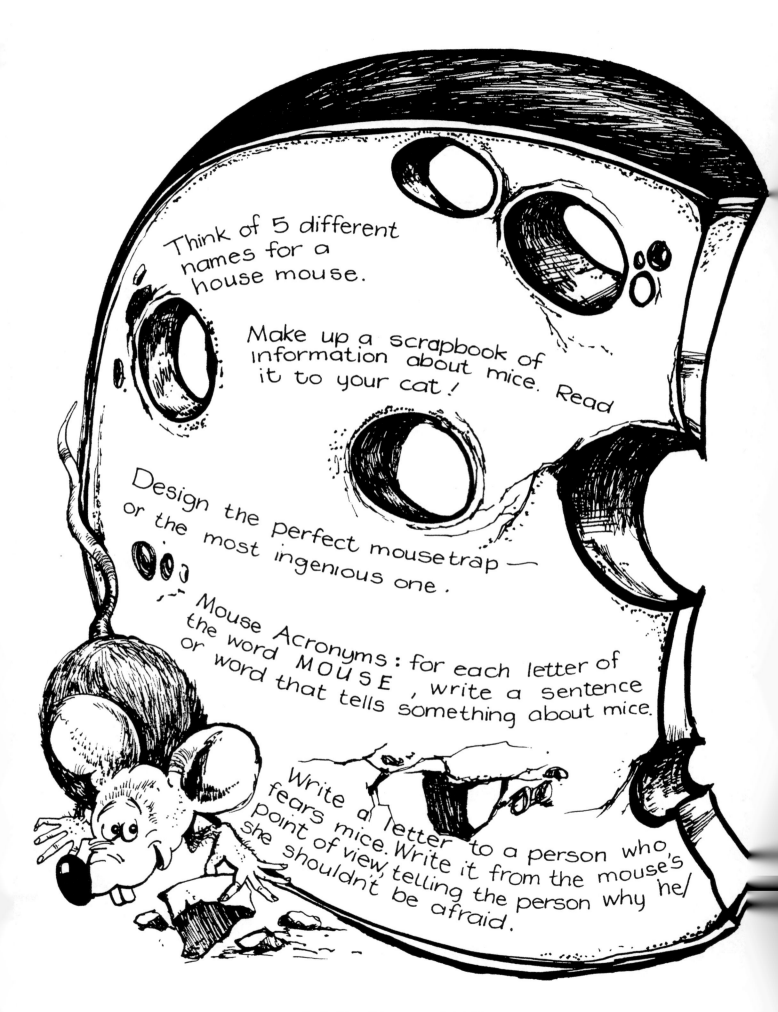

Think of 5 different names for a house mouse.

Make up a scrapbook of information about mice. Read it to your cat!

Design the perfect mousetrap — or the most ingenious one.

Mouse Acronyms: for each letter of the word M O U S E, write a sentence or word that tells something about mice.

Write a letter to a person who fears mice. Write it from the mouse's point of view, telling the person why he/she shouldn't be afraid.

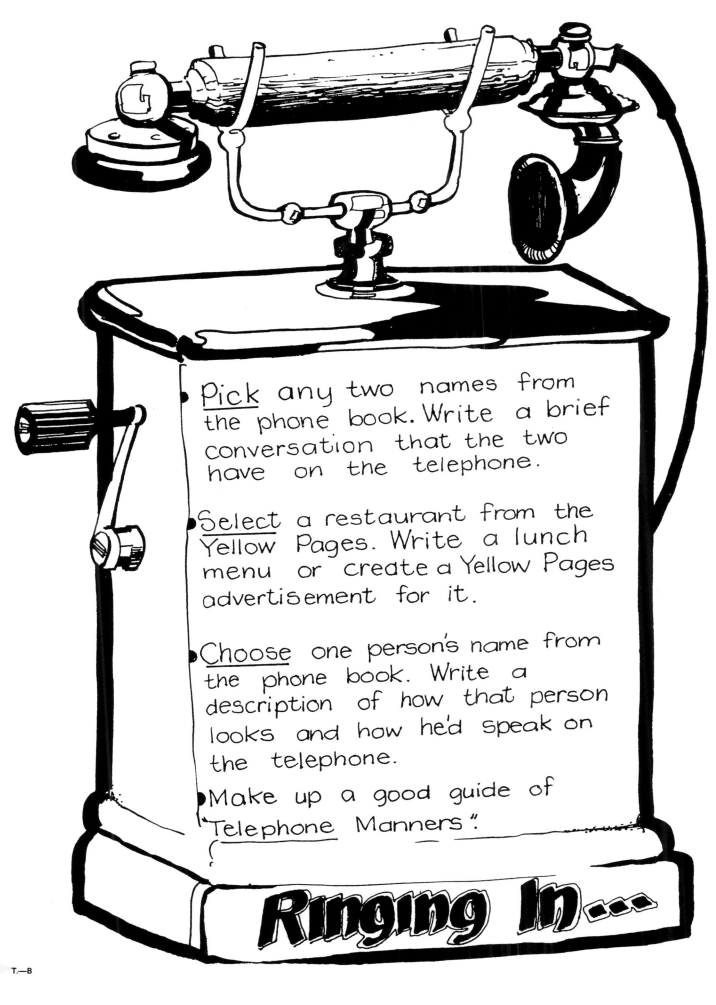

- <u>Pick</u> any two names from the phone book. Write a brief conversation that the two have on the telephone.

- <u>Select</u> a restaurant from the Yellow Pages. Write a lunch menu or create a Yellow Pages advertisement for it.

- <u>Choose</u> one person's name from the phone book. Write a description of how that person looks and how he'd speak on the telephone.

- Make up a good guide of "Telephone Manners".

Ringing In...

T.—B

Rubbish Reckonings

- Build up a glossary of rubbish-related words, terms and phrases.

- For each letter of the word ... GARBAGE, write a word that could describe it.

- Write a job description for a Garbologist. Make a list of the required duties.

- Choose one piece of trash. Write sentences describing each of its characteristics, i.e. its shape, size, texture, colour and use.

- Write the conversation between two lunch-time pieces of rubbish.

- Write a revolting rubbish rhyme

- Create a bumper sticker encouraging people not to litter.

Ship Ahoy!

1) Dip into the treasure chest filled with interesting things, Take one object and tell of its story.

2) Write your own sea shanty with a strong, repetitive chorus!

3) Write & send a ransom note, from blood-thirsty pirates.

5) Write the ship's log, containing entries of when the vessel was attacked by pirates.

4) Design a treasure map. Write the instructions for finding the buried treasure Tear the edges & stain wi cold tea for extr effect!

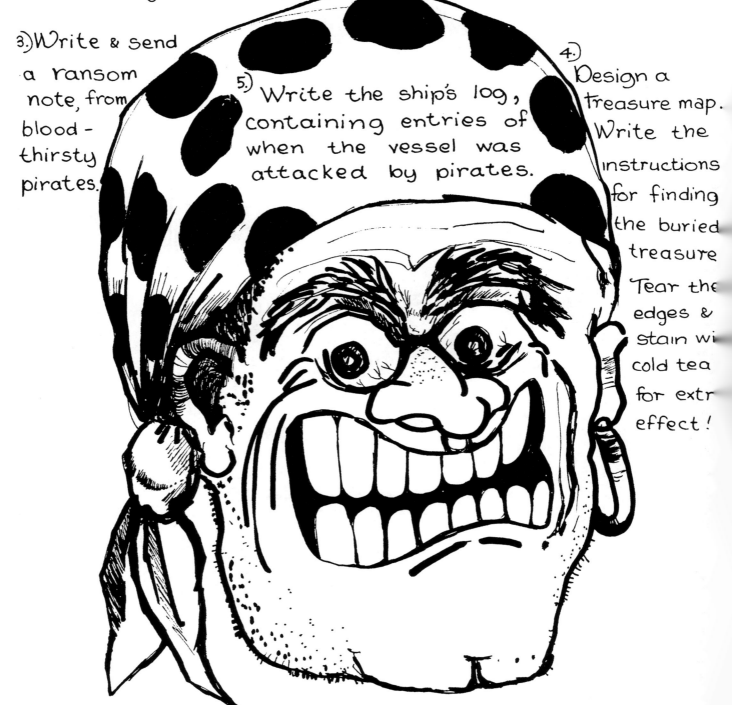

• List the contents of your buried treasure chest!

Time & Time Again ...

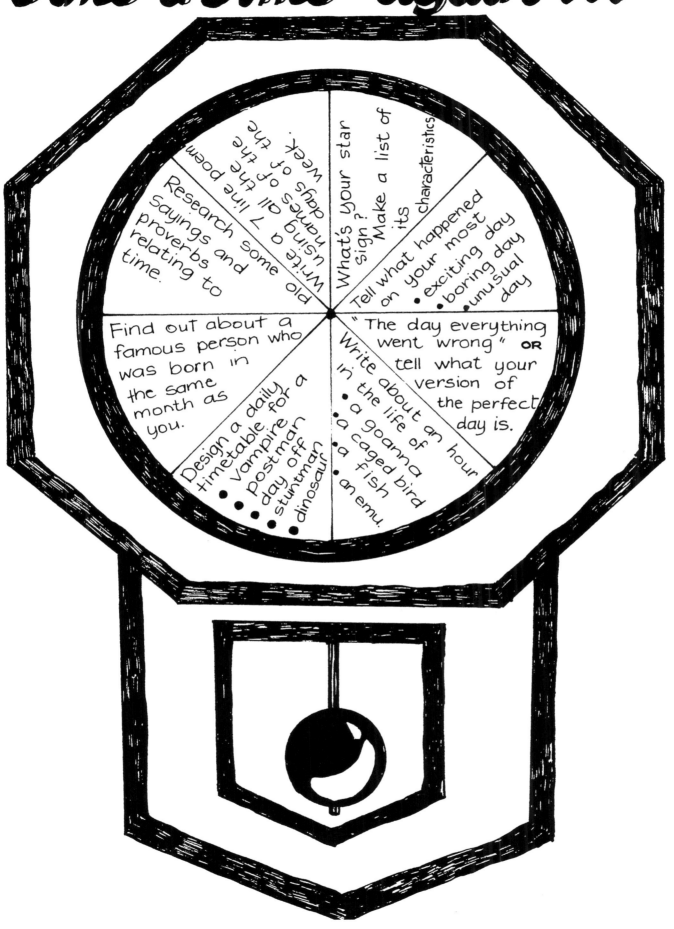

What's your star sign? Make a list of its characteristics.

Tell what happened on your most
• exciting day
• boring day
• unusual day

"The day everything went wrong" **OR** tell what your version of the perfect day is.

Write about an hour in the life of
• a goanna
• a caged bird
• a fish
• an emu.

Design a daily timetable for a
• vampire
• postman
• day off
• stuntman
• dinosaur

Find out about a famous person who was born in the same month as you.

Research some old sayings and proverbs relating to time.

Write a 7 line poem using all the names of the days of the week.

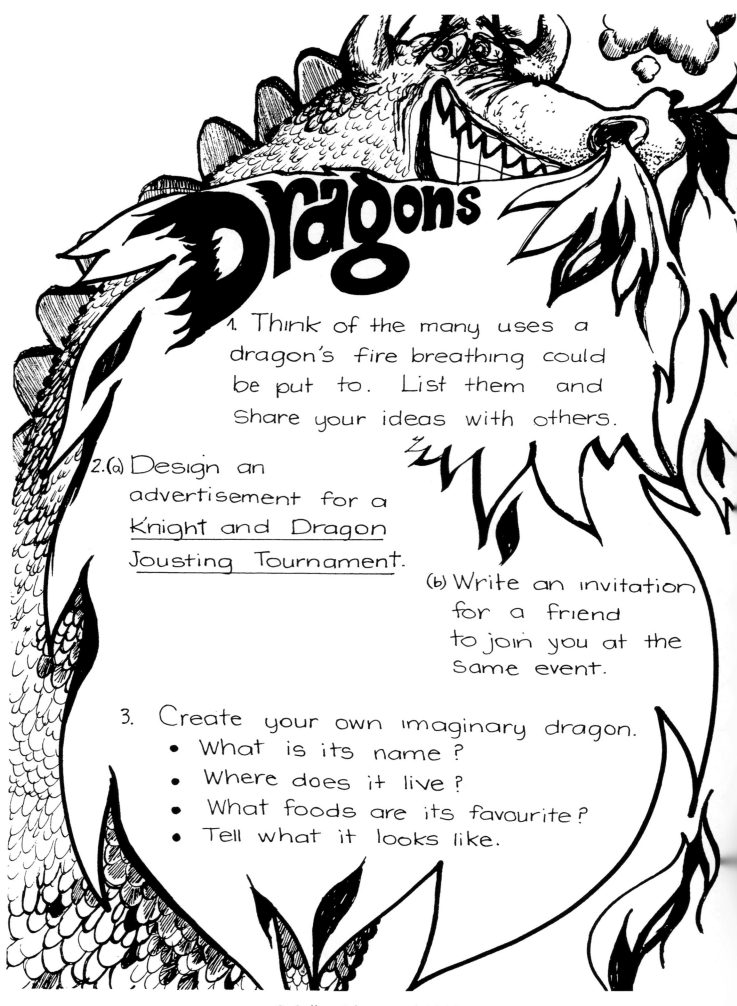

Dragons

1. Think of the many uses a dragon's fire breathing could be put to. List them and share your ideas with others.

2. (a) Design an advertisement for a <u>Knight and Dragon Jousting Tournament</u>.

   (b) Write an invitation for a friend to join you at the same event.

3. Create your own imaginary dragon.
   - What is its name?
   - Where does it live?
   - What foods are its favourite?
   - Tell what it looks like.

Write recipes for meals based on bones.

eg. Jumbuck Shanks.
  Bacon Bone Broth.
  Oxtail Soup.
  Kangaroo Tail Stew.
  Tough Tusk Rusks.

Reporting in...

Describe the fight between two prehistoric creatures, as an on-the-spot television reporter would view it.

Write a <u>skeleton story</u> (a brief outline) about a specific prehistoric bird or animal.

BONES

You snap the wishbone of a chicken and make a wish. Suddenly, everything becomes hazy ... Your wish is coming true!

<u>Tell about it</u>

animal crackers

Elephantine means like an elephant. What do these words mean?

canine _____

serpentine _____

vulturine _____

feline _____

bovine _____

Draw the head of an animal. Fold the paper under so that only the neck can be seen. Pass it to your partner, who, without looking at the head, draws a body on the neck. Fold this under too. Pass on to another person who draws the legs.

Unfold, and think of a crazy name for your character!

Make up a "Be On The Lookout" poster, describing an animal who is missing from the zoo. Tell of the animal's appearance and suggest the types of places he may be lurking in.

What sorts of animals make these movements?

waddle _____

strut _____

prowl _____

lope _____

glide _____

Collect animal expressions. What do these mean?

catty _____

doe-eyed _____

dog eared _____

monkey business _____

_____

Sheepish. _____

Scene on Camp

Write the conversation between two of your exhausted camping boots!

Write an advertisement for a tent, as it might appear in
* a children's magazine.
* a women's magazine.

Climb into your sleeping bag.. How does it feel? Describe the colour, texture and fit.

Finish these similes.
My sleeping bag is as cosy as _____.
and feels like _____:
It is as warm as _____.

Write about the strange dream you experienced last night.

Report the conversation between two sleeping bag zippers, one steel the other nylon.

c

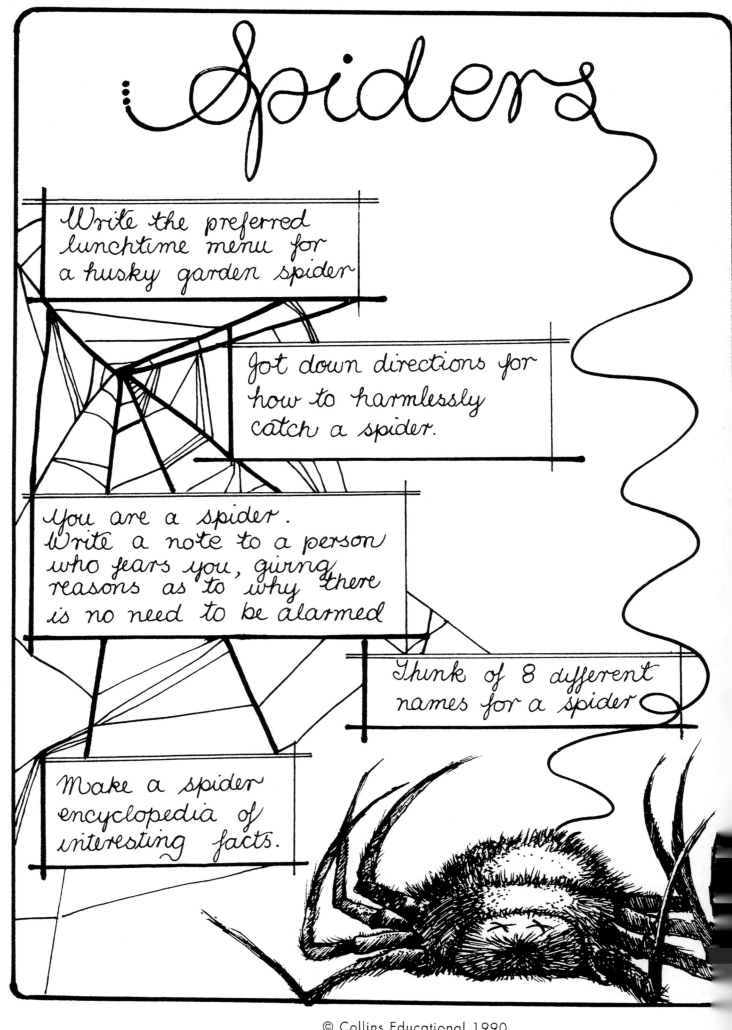

Spiders

Write the preferred lunchtime menu for a husky garden spider

Jot down directions for how to harmlessly catch a spider.

You are a spider. Write a note to a person who fears you, giving reasons as to why there is no need to be alarmed

Think of 8 different names for a spider

Make a spider encyclopedia of interesting facts.

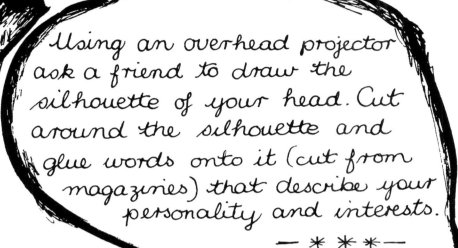

Using an overhead projector ask a friend to draw the silhouette of your head. Cut around the silhouette and glue words onto it (cut from magazines) that describe your personality and interests.

— * * * —

Draw around your hand, cut around this, and write your favourite recipe in the palm.

youniquely you

Write a <u>resumé</u> of your qualifications to be
· a champion sportsman,
· a clown,
· a disc jockey,
· a lion tamer,
· a stuntman/woman.

Write a <u>character</u> <u>reference</u> for your pet dog, cat or budgie!

...YOUR NOSE KNOWS ...

WRITE AN ADVERTISEMENT FOR A NEW DEODORANT ON THE MARKET!

DESIGN THE CAN AND DESCRIBE THE ACTIVE INGREDIENTS!!

Invent a new perfume.
Describe the aroma,
the ingredients,
the cost,
the best place and
time to wear the
new scent.

Use interesting words to describe the smell of:
* Salt and pepper.
* Cheese.
* the inside of a rubbish bin.
* mothballs.

Create a colourful collage of cut out words from perfume and cologne advertisements.
Read it to the class.

Write an exciting description of the most scrumptious dessert you can imagine!

Date: _____

Today's Special Dessert ~ Chef's Suggestion.

_____

_____
_____
_____
_____
_____
_____
_____
_____
_____
_____
_____

Today's Price is : _____

Sample a crunchy apple in class

- Give one word describing how the apple <u>looks</u>.
- Shut your eyes, run your fingers over the outer skin, give one word about how it <u>feels to touch</u>.
- Take a bite: ...
  - describe the <u>sound</u> as your teeth sink in
  - how does it <u>taste</u>?
  (Be accurate: floury? crisp? sweet? juicy?)
- Swallow ...
- Give one sentence that describes how it <u>leaves your mouth feeling</u>.

- List your apple tasting sensations one under the other ...

<u>Yippee</u>!! - Instant Poetry!!

Apple.
Appealing,
Slippery,
Crunchy,
Crisp,
It makes my tongue tingle.

Write your poems on apple-shaped paper. Glue all poems onto a large class chart, making an apple vocab tree.

——————————

* ~ It's a simple, fun way to build up vocabulary charts for the room. ~ *

——————————

Try the same with: lemons, celery, grapes, honey or any seasonal veges or fruits

HUNGER PANGS!

Design an advertising campaign for one of the following restaurants:

(1 Sandwich Salon.
(2 Crepe Souls.
(3 Jaffle Joint.
(4 Waffle World.
(5 Yogurt Bar.

(6 Sausage Skin.
(7 Avocado Nut.
(8 The Pie Cabin.
(9 Steak Cave.
(10 Hamburger Haven.

———★———

(a. Think of a name for the restaurant.
(b. Write either the lunch or dinner menu.
      (use heaps of tasty words!)
(c. Make up a radio jingle or plan and act out a T.V. advertisement.

When planning your advert take into consideration which angle (or selling point) you are going to use to encourage people to visit your restaurant.
eg: the price factor, intimate atmosphere, give-aways, types of food, quality of service etc

A BOX OF
BIX

- Eating Bix makes you healthy and strong, So eat more Bix you can't go _____ . It's just so crunchy and _____ too,

_____

_____ .

(finish the poem & sing it as a radio ad.)

- Make up a tongue twister selecting from some of these words _____ ...

  crispy, crunchy, crackly, non fattening, fibrous, filling.

- Tell of the time you found weevils in the Bix box!

- Write a letter to the manufacturer of Bix telling of your dissatisfaction with his product.

- Write his reply.

Ideas

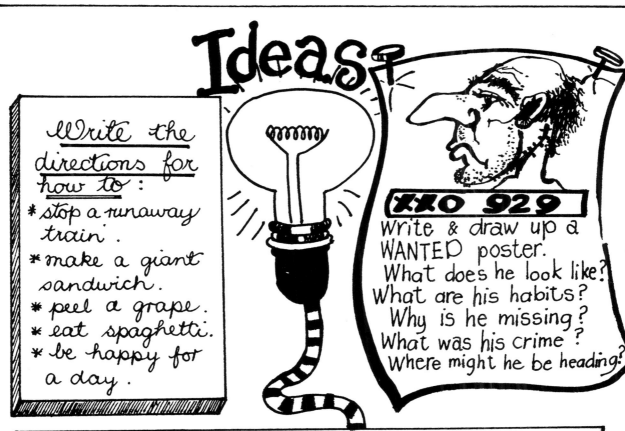

Write the directions for how to:
* stop a runaway train.
* make a giant sandwich.
* peel a grape.
* eat spaghetti.
* be happy for a day.

XXO 929

Write & draw up a WANTED poster.
What does he look like?
What are his habits?
Why is he missing?
What was his crime?
Where might he be heading?

Write **5** reasons
• for laughing.
• why bananas should have zippers.
• for not doing homework.
• for pickled onions.

Please Come

• Extend an invitation • to someone. State

TO: FROM: TIME: DATE:

OCCASION:

use your imagination!

• go on a snake hunt
• venture on a balloon ride
• a chance to meet Captain Cook!
• a trip up a rugged mountain.

SECRETS

Write secret messages with lemon juice, apple juice or vinegar.

Pass the secret message on to someone else.

The message can be deciphered by holding the paper close to a hot light or by ironing with a warm iron. The writing will turn brown.

Shhhh

CRAFTY CHARACTERS...

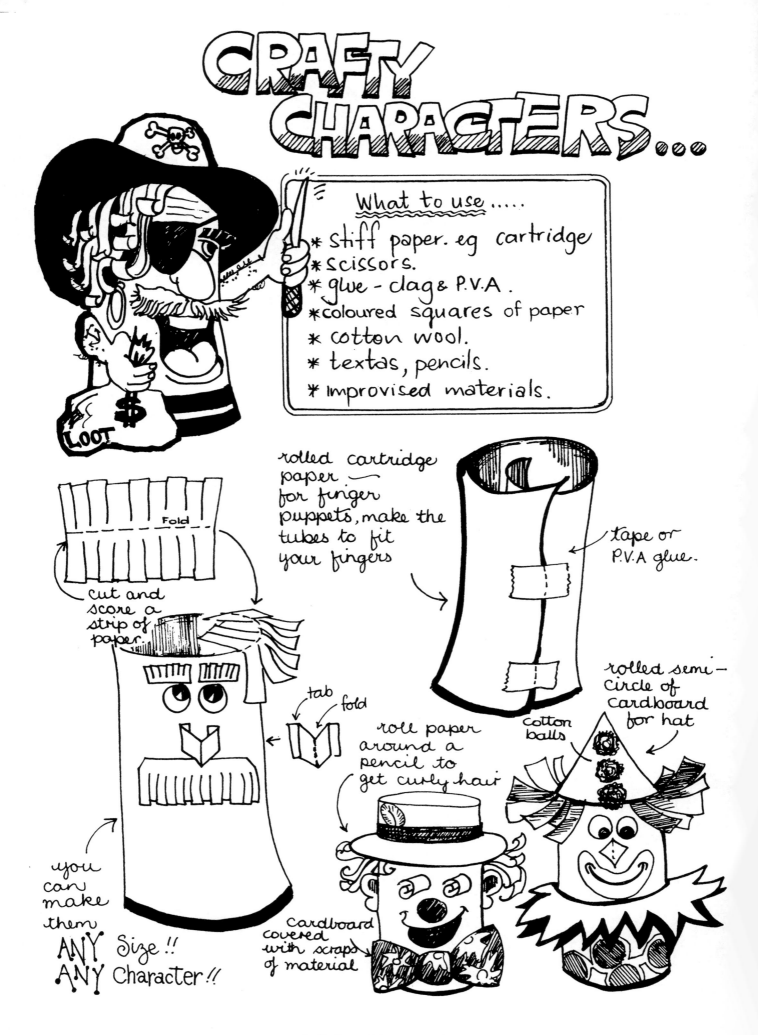

What to use .....
* stiff paper. eg cartridge
* scissors.
* glue - clag & P.V.A.
* coloured squares of paper
* cotton wool.
* textas, pencils.
* improvised materials.

rolled cartridge paper - for finger puppets, make the tubes to fit your fingers

tape or P.V.A glue.

Fold

cut and score a strip of paper.

tab fold

roll paper around a pencil to get curly hair

rolled semi-circle of cardboard for hat

cotton balls

you can make them ANY Size !! ANY Character !!

Cardboard covered with scraps of material

These crafty little characters may be used to stimulate creative writing, drama & oral English. They also provide an attractive classroom display !!

Encourage diversity of characters — select from some of these ....

Doctor.	Grave digger	Gangster.
Dentist.	Movie Star.	Jockey.
Lion Tamer.	Rock singer.	Surfer.
Magician.	Nurse.	Sailor.
Farrier	Zoo Keeper.	Musician.
Gardener.	Teacher.	Gambler.
Burglar.	Garbage man.	Butcher.
Editor.	Principal.	Chef.
Builder	Mechanic.	Disc jockey.	Artist.
Prime Minister.	Cleaner.	Clown.	Carpenter.
Sportsman.	Fisherman.	Hypnotist.	Scientist.

Discuss & decide what type of character you'd prefer to be....

List all the characteristics relating to your model —

eg: Pirate: eye patch, bag for loot, knife, sword scars, moustache, sneaky mouth

After models have been constructed —

Write a poem, or paragraph from your character's point of view ...
- What's your name? Address?
- What's your personality like?
- What do you like most & least about your job right now?

In groups of 3 or 4, make up puppet plays for other classes.

Eventually, hang characters as class mobiles.

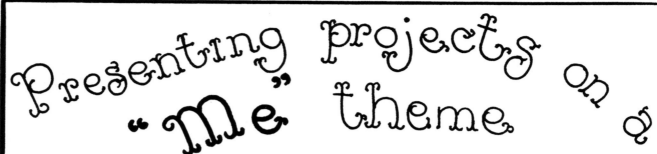

Presenting projects on a "Me" theme

1. <u>Cut out life-sized silhouette of child & glue all the information onto this.</u>

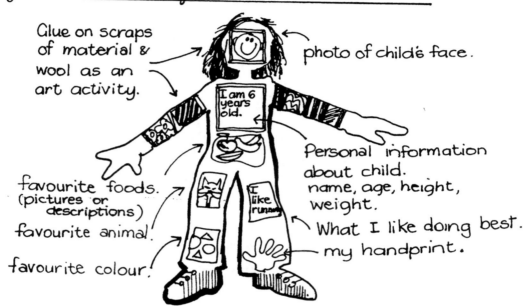

Glue on scraps of material & wool as an art activity.

photo of child's face.

I am 6 years old.

favourite foods. (pictures or descriptions)

favourite animal.

favourite colour.

Personal information about child. name, age, height, weight.

What I like doing best.

my handprint.

2. <u>Memory Cubes</u> - information is glued onto an empty carton & suspended at touchable height

pictures can be glued onto an empty milk carton.

Each side of the cube can display a different facet of the child's character, likes, dislikes, favourite things etc.

Project Books

individual

Me Myself and I

Sally

A personal record of the child.

5.6.82
My name is Linda.
I live in Geraldton at 5 Smith Street
I have two brothers. Their names are Ian...

or class books

I am Joanne I am 7 years old When I grow up, I want to be a plumber.

and swimming

My name is Paul.
My favourite thing is playing cricket with my friend Jeremy. We have two big dogs to look after our house.
Here is Sometimes I like to look at the shells at the beach and make castles.

Each child's piece of work is compiled into a class book.
..... Great to give to new classmembers to take home and read.

– Memory Cubes –

I am 7 yrs old and I like eating icecreams.

Debra

SUSPEND FROM ONE EDGE SO THAT ALL FACES CAN BE SEEN.

* A photograph of child, personal data about self and family and pets.

* A favourite colour, smells, tastes, sports, sights, hobbies, interests, clothes, animals, places, foods, pop stars.

* Handprint, footprint, fingerprint

* Texture one side with cotton wool or sandpaper.

* Write your first memory, tell about a funny time or remember a sad occasion.

All Sorts of good ideas!

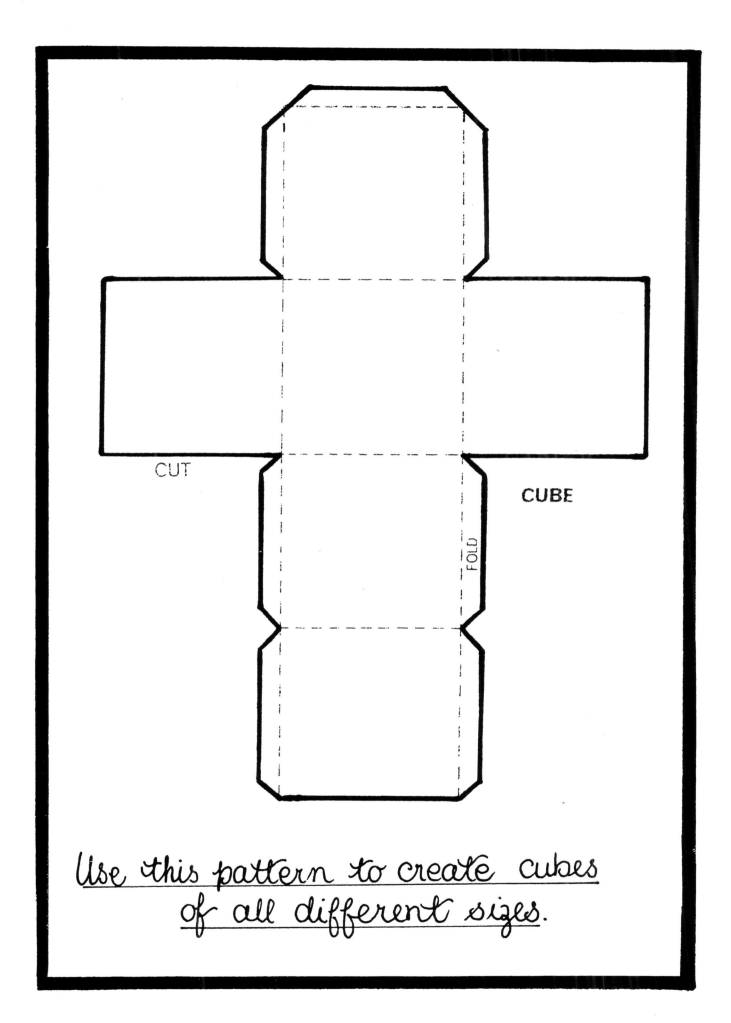

CUT

CUBE

FOLD

Use this pattern to create cubes
of all different sizes.

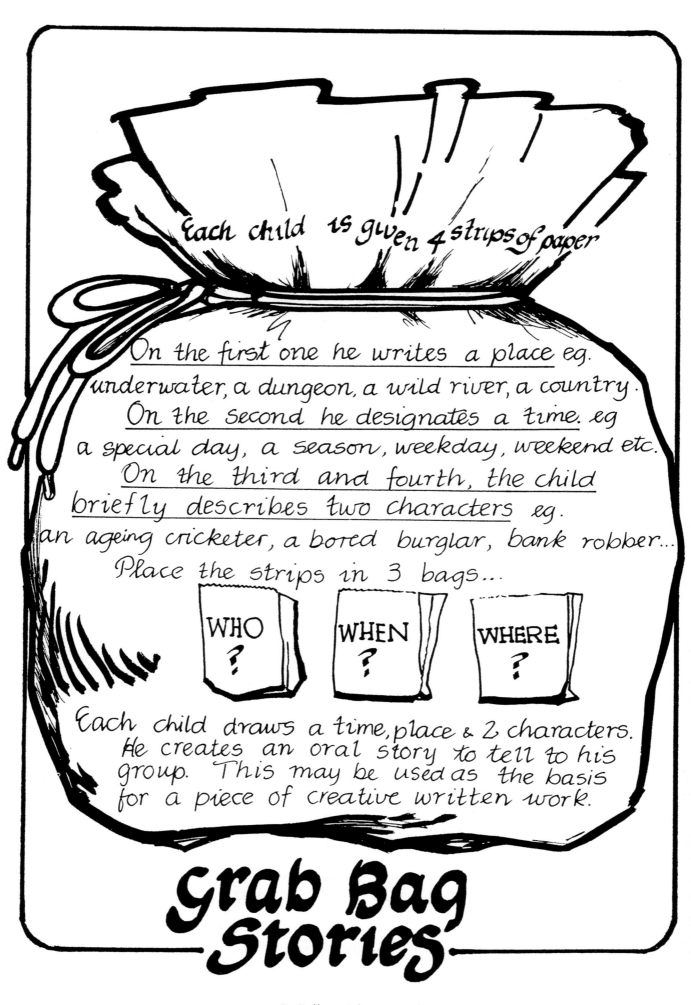

Each child is given 4 strips of paper

On the first one he writes a place eg. underwater, a dungeon, a wild river, a country. On the second he designates a time. eg a special day, a season, weekday, weekend etc. On the third and fourth, the child briefly describes two characters eg. an ageing cricketer, a bored burglar, bank robber...

Place the strips in 3 bags...

WHO ?

WHEN ?

WHERE ?

Each child draws a time, place & 2 characters. He creates an oral story to tell to his group. This may be used as the basis for a piece of creative written work.

Grab Bag Stories

SPELLS:

Write the magical words which must be spoken,

1.) to make the school day pass more quickly.
2.) to enable a person to become invisible.
3.) so that you can have X-ray vision instantly.
4.) to travel back into time.

Horror-Scopes

Find out your star sign...

... predict events which will happen for you during the following week.

Changing Forms

I'd like to be a _____ because
(name of an animal)

_____

_____

_____

Some of the reasons I'd like to be a
_____ are because _____
(name of a plant)

_____

_____

Main Parts of a Newspaper

1.) <u>Editorial</u>. (the newspaper's official opinion)

2.) <u>Letters</u>. (readers' opinions)

3.) <u>News stories</u>. (information)

4.) <u>Sports stories</u>.

5.) <u>Features</u>. (fashion, cookery, motoring, literary, gardens.)

6.) <u>Cartoon</u>. (comment & amusement)

7.) <u>Comic strips</u>. (amusement)

8.) <u>Advertisements</u>. (persuasion)

9.) Weather & other services.

<u>Find one example of each of the above types of articles.</u>

Which comic strip character do you enjoy the most?

_____

What is today's editorial about?

_____

_____

What do most of to-day's Letters to the Editor seem to be about? _____

_____

GETTING INTO PRINT

1. Name one newspaper which is printed daily and distributed
a. Over the whole state.

b. Over the whole of Australia.

2. What do we call a "local rag"?

3. Name two magazines which are directed at women.   a. _____.
b. _____.

4. What are some of the differences between a newspaper and a magazine?

5. Name one magazine which is concerned with current affairs. _____.

6. When people have finished reading a newspaper, what generally happens to it?

RESEARCH

1. Who sends in Letters to the Editor?

   _____

2. What is a <u>back copy</u> of a newspaper or a magazine?

   _____

3. Where would you be likely to obtain a back copy?

   _____

4. What is the Editor's job?

   _____

5. What does a journalist do?

   _____

6. Select a magazine (eg "Women's Weekly").
   Calculate the percentage of space given to advertising in the magazine.
   Use this formula...

   $$\frac{\text{Number of full page ads}}{\text{Total number of pages}} \times \frac{100}{1} = \boxed{}\%$$

7. Why do you think there are so many advertisements in your magazine?

   _____

   _____

8. What has the most influence on <u>You</u> — radio, newspapers or television? _____

CLASSIFY

In groups of 3 or 4 use a current newspaper to find and cut out articles on the following ...

An accident report.	A comic strip.
An international news item.	A birth/death notice.
A letter to the editor.	A sporting item.
A book/film/theatre review.	A crime report.
A report on Government policy.	Business news.

Note the page number on which the articles appear and, using a large sheet of paper, print the newspaper's <u>name</u> and <u>date</u> in bold heading at the top.

Glue and label your articles onto it.
Use sub-headings for the different sections.

— phew; I think next term we'll go back to watching T.V. Broadcasts !!

Telegrams to go...

```
┌─────────────────────────────────────────────────────────────────┐
│  ┌──────────────┐                                    ◉ Telecom    │
│  │ TELEGRAM     │                                      Australia. │
│  └──────────────┘                                                 │
│  P                                                                │
│  L   TO _____                           │
│  E   _____                            │
│  A   _____ STATE ___  REMEMBER: Telegrams     │
│  S   _____    addressed to a          │
│  E   _____    telephone or telex      │
│  U   _____    number can SAVE         │
│  S   _____    MONEY and SPEED         │
│  E   _____    DELIVERY.               │
│  B   _____                            │
│  L   _____                            │
│  O   FROM (For Transmission) _____                           │
│  C   ─────────────────────────────────                           │
│  K   NOT FOR TRANSMISSION                                         │
│  L   SENDER'S NAME _____ TELEPHONE NO. _____            │
│  E   ADDRESS _____                           │
│  T   (For Contact if required)                                    │
│  R                                                                │
│  S                                                                │
└─────────────────────────────────────────────────────────────────┘
```

1. Send a telegram from our Prime Minister congratulating a famous sportsman/woman.
2. Write a telegram to the gardener from an over watered plant.
3. Send one from a lion to its tamer.
4. Or one from a dog to the cat next door.
5. Send one from the dentist to your mother.

1. Write what the diver is thinking.
2. What does the shark think?
3. What is your solution to the problem?

What helpful hints is she giving to him?

Write the directions
for how to get
peanut butter off the
roof of your mouth!

CHOPSTIX CONNECTIONS!

Write a set of instructions for how to eat B.B.Q sausages with a pair of chopsticks.

1. Write what the dentist is saying.

2. What is she thinking?

What do you think she is saying? Write it, then act it out